CREATE YOUR OWN MIDLIFE CRISIS

CREATE YOUR OWN
MIDLIFE CRISIS

The Best Way to Make the Worst Decisions

MARIE PHILLIPS

CHRONICLE PRISM

First published in the United States of America in 2021 by Chronicle Books LLC. Originally published in the United Kingdom in 2019 by Souvenir Press, an imprint of Profile Books Ltd.

Library of Congress Cataloging-in-Publication Data
Names: Phillips, Marie, 1976—author.
Title: Create your own midlife crisis : the best way to make the worst
    decisions / Marie Phillips.
Description: San Francisco : Chronicle Prism, 2021.
Identifiers: LCCN 2020042857 | ISBN 9781797207100 (hardcover) | ISBN
    9781797207124 (ebook)
Subjects: LCSH: Midlife crisis—Humor. | Middle-aged persons—Humor. |
    Decision making—Humor. | Plot-your-own stories.
Classification: LCC PN6231.M47 P55 2021 | DDC 818/.602—dc23
LC record available at https://lccn.loc.gov/2020042857

Manufactured in China.

Cover design by Lindsey Cleworth.
Illustrations by Lindsey Cleworth.
Interior design by Pamela Geismar.
Typesetting by Maureen Forys, Happenstance Type-O-Rama.
Typeset in Citrus Gothic and Futura.

10 9 8 7 6 5 4 3 2 1

Chronicle books and gifts are available at special quantity discounts to corporations, professional associations, literacy programs, and other organizations. For details and discount information, please contact our premiums department at corporatesales@chroniclebooks.com or at 1-800-759-0190.

CHRONICLE PRISM

Chronicle Prism is an imprint of Chronicle Books LLC, 680 Second Street, San Francisco, California 94107
www.chronicleprism.com

Midway through the journey of our life
I found myself within a dark wood
Where the straight path had been lost.

—Dante Alighieri, *The Divine Comedy*

This is a book unlike any other, particularly any that is under copyright. Instead of following a storyline set for you by the author, YOU are the creator of your own destiny.

You are a woman in midlife, with a husband, a daughter, and a successful career, but the nagging sense that something is missing.

You will need all your intelligence and ingenuity as you weave your way through the perilous midlife maze, with DANGER at every turn. Will you:

Sext your married colleague?
Get a very small tattoo?
Go to a nightclub with your mother?
Run away to Brazil?

YOU DECIDE.

You have nothing to lose except your marriage, your career, and your self-respect.

It's a Friday morning. You are in a meeting. By your estimate, this meeting has been going on for 472 years. By your watch, it has been going on for nineteen minutes. There is one hour and forty-one minutes left to go. Your boss is presenting a sales strategy that you have already had seven meetings about and that will be changed beyond recognition the moment it is sent up to her boss. To your left, a junior account executive keeps sniffling—huge, wet sniffles that sound like an elephant snorting molasses. To your right is Hot Russell, who you nearly kissed once at an offsite meeting in Iowa City before remembering that you are both married. Hot Russell is stifling a yawn and checking a text message under the table. As he looks up, you catch his eye.

⋯⋯⋙ If you want to write a message to Hot Russell, turn to 131.

⋯⋯⋙ If you want to tell your boss that this meeting is a waste of everybody's time, turn to 4.

⋯⋯⋙ If you want to give the junior account executive a tissue, turn to 83.

"What do you do?" asks the man with multiple piercings who smells of wheat. He has a Brazilian accent.

You explain, in some detail, the boring office job that you used to do before you decided to run away to Brazil. You notice that the very little, very old lady sitting on the other side of you is falling asleep.

"How about you?" you say eventually.

"I'm a shaman."

You experience some regret about how much detail you decided to go into about, for example, spreadsheets.

The man with the piercings explains that he runs ayahuasca ceremonies for tourists (only he doesn't say "tourists," he says "discerning travelers") in the Amazon jungle. "It is a very profound spiritual experience," he says. "A precious rite of passage. I can let you do it for free if you'll teach me how to use Excel. I really struggle with the bookkeeping, because I'm high almost all of the time."

Maybe all that spreadsheet talk wasn't such a bad idea.

⋯⋯⟩ To take the shaman up on his offer, turn to 117.

⋯⋯⟩ To take your chances on your own in Brazil, turn to 151.

"No thanks," you tell your dad.

"Why not?" says your dad. "It'll be fun! We'll match!"

You run through all the possible answers in your head. Because you don't like tattoos. Because you are worried that you will look ridiculous with a tattoo when you are old. Because you are scared that it will hurt. None of these are things that you can say to your father, who has just gotten a tattoo himself.

"Oh, OK then," you say. "I'll get a tattoo."

"That's my girl!"

You add this to the lengthy list of things you really didn't want to do that your dad has pressured you into over the years, including eating liver, swimming in the Atlantic Ocean in February, and having dinner with the son of that friend of his from work.

······⟩ Turn to 147.

Shaking, you get to your feet. Your boss stops speaking and puts the lid back on the magic marker she was using to draw a completely pointless graph. The click of the lid is impossibly loud.

"Yes?" she says.

"Cheryl," you say. "I think I speak for all of us when I say that if I spend another second in this meeting my brain is going to melt and dribble out of my ears."

"She doesn't speak for me," says the junior account executive.

"That's because your brain is already coming out of your nose," you say.

"Are you feeling OK?" says Cheryl.

Are you feeling OK? It is a good question. Your husband has been warning you for a while that you've been working too hard and are heading for burnout. Maybe this is burnout. Or maybe you just really hate your job.

⋯⋯⋗ To apologize to your boss, turn to 135.

⋯⋯⋗ To tell your boss where to shove her job, turn to 24.

Hot Russell stands up. "I need to make a report of sexual harassment in the workplace," he says.

He hands his phone with the topless picture on it to your boss. Your boss looks at it, her face going pale. As you await your fate, your predicament is made yet worse by noticing that she has much nicer boobs than yours.

"I think you and I had better step into my office," your boss says to you. "The rest of you can go. I'll get Agatha to reschedule the meeting."

You notice the sniffly junior account executive and the vice president of marketing giving each other a surreptitious high five. They have probably bonded by both having faulty noses, you think.

Your boss leads the way to her office. You follow her. For a crazy moment, it occurs to you that you could just run away into the street. That's insane, you think. What kind of a person would run away from their office into the street?

⋯⋯▷ To run away from your office into the street, turn to 141.

⋯⋯▷ To follow your boss into her office, turn to 26.

"You are wrong," you write.

Seconds later, you get a reply. "No," it says, "YOU are wrong."

⋯⋯▷ To let this go, turn to 109.

⋯⋯▷ To reply, turn to 113.

7

Your boss is still babbling on about something but you are paying even less attention to it than usual as you wait for your husband's response.

Toss a coin!

If you get heads, turn to 106.

If you get tails, turn to 130.

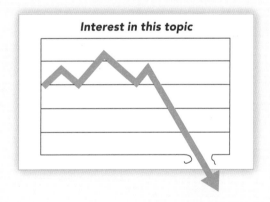

Interest in this topic

You don't need a stockbroker! You can figure it out for yourself. How hard can it be? You do more research and decide to put all your money into a cryptocurrency called Gull-E-Ball.

You get regular emails telling you that the value of your investment is going up and up and up. Your husband quits his job and you make plans to take your daughter out of school and spend a year traveling around the world together. In the meantime you become extravagant: You start dry cleaning your dry-clean-only clothing instead of shoving it in the machine on the delicates cycle and hoping for the best.

When the time comes to cash in your Gull-E-Balls, the website has disappeared. The only trace you can find that Gull-E-Balls ever existed is a reference to it in an "obvious scams" subreddit.

You and your husband are both unemployed. All of your money is gone. At least your dry cleaner greets you by name, but you wonder how you ended up here.

You shave your head. It looks terrible. You have one of those skulls that is covered in knobby lumps that look like you were crafted from clay and then whoever did it stuck the leftover pieces on and just squished them down a bit.

You are a middle-aged woman who looks like a Sinéad O'Connor impersonator, without the extraordinary singing talent or the complicated feelings about the pope. Your scalp is very cold. You wonder how you ended up here.

You open up LinkedIn and sync your contacts, but it takes you so long to locate and remove all of your ex-boyfriends from the "connect with people you know" screen that you give up and shut it down again.

·····⟩ To look up get-rich-quick schemes, turn to 98.

·····⟩ To give up on the whole thing and start scrolling through Twitter, turn to 122.

You follow the man in his latex fetish suit into a private room. It smells of cheap pine air freshener and whatever the air freshener was trying to disguise. There is a large plastic mattress in the corner. Next to it is a box of wet wipes with a picture of a smiling baby on it, and a Blu-tacked sign reading "Please clean up all bodily waste."

"Great," says mystery latex-man. "Help me out of this suit."

You unzip the suit. When you remove the mask, you realize that you *do* recognize this man.

Toss a coin!

······⟩ If you get heads, turn to 136.

······⟩ If you get tails, turn to 48.

You suggest meeting your husband on neutral territory, so after work you get together at a neighborhood bar where once the only customers were old men reading the sports pages but where they now sell sixty types of gin to hipsters with directional hairstyles. You both agree that you need to take drastic action to save your marriage.

⋯⋯➢ To work through your differences in couples therapy, turn to 138.

⋯⋯➢ To distract yourselves from your differences, why not take on an exciting new project together! Your kitchen has been crying out for a renovation for ages—now's your chance. Turn to 73.

You enter the yoga space. There is a statue of Buddha at the front of the room and a candle that smells like bathroom cleaner. Everyone is wearing branded athleisure gear except for you. You are wearing the T-shirt and leggings you use for (occasional) running, (occasional) housework, and (frequent) sitting on the couch watching television.

The teacher appears. He is an extremely hairy man. The only relief from the hair are his eyes and his tiny shorts and ultra-tight tank top. He tests his headset microphone: "One. Two. One. Two. Namaste. Namaste." Then he begins the class.

"Everyone sit in lotus position. Inhale. Exhale. Now lift your foot onto your elbow. Now onto your shoulder. Now put it behind your head."

Toss a coin!

┈┈┈⫶⟩ Heads, turn to 120.

┈┈┈⫶⟩ Tails, turn to 154.

14

You can't face going through all of that again. Just the thought of that horrible doctor's hairy knuckles is enough to make you sit with your legs crossed for the rest of your life. But you need something to help you move on. Some kind of change.

┄┄┄▷ To change your inner self, turn to 72.

┄┄┄▷ To change your outer self, turn to 81.

"I actually need to speak to her urgently outside," says Hot Russell. "I've just noticed a discrepancy in the figures. I don't want to disrupt the meeting any further." His hand brushes against your thigh. You really hope that hot feeling wasn't a UTI.

"Alright then," says your boss. "If you must. Try not to take too long."

"We'll make it a quickie," says Hot Russell.

You both get up and walk out of the meeting. Your heart is pounding, your legs are weak, and your wedding ring suddenly feels extremely tight on your finger.

"Ladies' or Gentlemen's?" says Hot Russell.

⤑ If the thought of having sex in a restroom is just unsexy enough to stop this, turn to 64.

⤑ If you are beyond the point of no return, turn to 31.

"I'm sorry," you say, "but the first rule of traveling is never to carry anybody else's bag through security."

"I understand," says the very little, very old, and very tired- and sad-sounding lady.

You walk slowly together through passport control. She grunts and groans as she heaves the trolley forward with all of her strength. Then, suddenly, the very little, very old lady stops. Her face turns gray; she sways and falls to the ground.

Airport personnel run over and try to resuscitate her, but it's no use. She's dead.

Now all of the very little, very old lady's children (other than the daughter in Rhode Island) and grandchildren and one adored great-grandson who had come to meet her at the airport surround the body and start weeping and wailing that they have lost their beloved mother/grandmother/great-grandmother. If only someone had been kind enough to help her with her bags, she might still be alive.

Someone points at you and all the relatives turn.

You are alone in an airport in Brazil and you've just killed a very little, very old lady and a lot of extremely angry people are shouting at you in Portuguese. You wonder how you ended up here.

Your log-in has not been rescinded yet, so you sit at an unobtrusive desk in the office surfing the internet looking for ways to make money and hoping nobody will notice you and throw you out of the building.

⸺⟩ To check LinkedIn, turn to 10.

⸺⟩ To look up get-rich-quick schemes, turn to 98.

⸺⟩ To give up on the whole thing and start scrolling through Twitter, turn to 122.

The guy gets a small Ziploc bag out of his pocket. It contains white powder. It could be anything from laundry detergent to cocaine to . . . other drugs that go up your nose. You haven't been in a club for so long you don't even *know* which drugs go up your nose. Bath salts? That's a thing now, right? You've read alarmist articles about them but you've never been entirely clear whether it's slang for something or whether people are actually snorting stuff they bought at Lush. You personally can't stand the smell of Lush products. You have to cross the street whenever you pass the shop. Can you ask this guy whether you can smell what's in the bag before you decide to take it? No. You definitely can't. You're just going to have to snort or not snort.

·····⟩ To snort: Turn to 57.

·····⟩ Or not to snort: Turn to 110.

The app now suggests BARTHOLOMEW. Bartholomew is dressed in full fox-hunting attire and is standing next to a horse. Around him there's a pack of beagles. In one hand he holds a whip and in the other, a headless fox by the tail. He lists his interests as climate change skepticism and exotic meats.

┈┈╌> Left for no? Turn to 86.

┈┈╌> Right for yes? Turn to 114.

20

You go through the same unpleasant process again, the same disquieting feeling that your future child's father is some goo in a cup, the same invasive insemination procedure, the same awful jokes—literally, the exact same ones—from the leering doctor, but this time, when you pee on the stick, you get a different result.

·······⋗ Turn to 152.

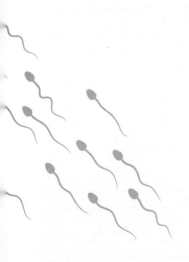

You sit with the other ritual participants (tourists) in the ceremonial space while the shaman distributes cups of ayahuasca tea, which tastes disgusting and would definitely be improved by having a cookie to dunk in it. You are not encouraged by the little buckets that he hands out with the tea. You know what they are for. The shaman starts singing, but soon enough you can't hear much over the sound of everyone throwing up.

You start to hallucinate. At first your mind is filled with visions of Excel spreadsheets, giant tropical spiders, and broken sofas that talk. Then the borders of your self start to slip away and you become one with the cosmos.

You float through the universe for a while, experiencing the true unity of all creation. Slowly you realize that the cosmos has a message for you.

The message is: Go home, you idiot.

You wonder how you ended up here.

Everybody at the airport is bored or angry. You feel right at home. You can't believe you never thought of running away from everything in your life sooner. You can't abandon your daughter, of course, but you'll send for her as soon as you are established in a beautiful, hot country with affordable childcare. In the meantime, it will be a good bonding experience for her to spend some time with her father for a change.

You scan the departure boards, looking for an appealing destination, a place where the weather is nice, the people are friendly, and you won't get dysentery.

Brazil! You buy your ticket. It costs a lot, but who cares? Life will be cheap in Brazil! (You have no idea whether life will be cheap in Brazil. You can't even name the currency of Brazil.)

You have three hours to kill before your flight leaves. You wander around the airport, browsing the overpriced shops and the cafés with seating that is supposed to resemble an al fresco terrace, the only difference being that you're either sitting inside a café inside an airport, or outside a café inside an airport.

You start to wonder whether you will miss your husband and daughter after all.

⋯⋯⋗ To go through with the plan, turn to 34.

⋯⋯⋗ To change your mind, turn to 32.

You have a boyfriend! Emphasis on boy. He is very sweet and devoted and indefatigable in the sack, but he doesn't understand anything you say. You have to give him a list of films and music to consume just so that you can share basic cultural references. You'd give him a book list too but he doesn't have the attention span to read.

After you've been together for a few months he introduces you to his parents. You recognize his mother. She was two years ahead of you in school. In fact you get along very well with her and you spend the entire meal quoting John Hughes movies at each other and you're having a great night until she reminds your boyfriend to finish his broccoli. You realize you should not have ended up here.

"You can shove your stupid job up your ass!" you yell at Cheryl. "I hate you! I hate all of you! Except you, Hot Russell, you are hot. Also, there is someone sitting there next to the vice president of marketing who I haven't met before and it is possible that you are a decent human being."

You wait for the person sitting next to the vice president of marketing to thank you, but they don't, so you carry on.

"I wouldn't piss on this job if it was on fire, and I know that doesn't make logical sense, and I don't care. I actually think that's quite a sexist expression because for a woman to piss on something that is on fire, she would have to squat quite low over it, and might become severely burned by the flames. In conclusion, up yours, I'm out of here!"

This triumphant valedictory speech is somehow less triumphant out loud than it sounded in your head, but never mind. You march out of the meeting room feeling amazing, a feeling that lasts entire seconds before you realize what you have done.

⸱⸱⸱⸱⸳> Turn to 108.

You can't quit. Your "kitchen" is a pile of broken bricks and wires and one old sink in the middle of the room that is neither your previous sink nor the sink you are getting, and nobody can explain how it got there. You have to keep going.

·····⟩ Turn to 51.

Your boss takes a seat behind her desk and you sit down opposite her. She taps her fingers together.

"Now listen," she says. "Obviously you have done a terrible thing, we take this extremely seriously, and so on. However. Firing you would not be great publicity for the firm. Also, losing you at this stage in the sales cycle would be highly problematic for my targets. But I have to show I'm doing something, so you'd better head off to Human Resources. Since Mildred retired, there's a bright young thing who is trying some . . . innovative approaches to helping people with burnout or behavioral difficulties, such as yourself."

⋯⋯⟩ To go to Human Resources, turn to 84.

⋯⋯⟩ To quit this stupid job, turn to 108.

You are in a Brazilian jail on charges of drug trafficking. Your court-appointed lawyer doesn't speak English. The American embassy keeps putting you on hold, and their choice of hold music is disgracefully bad bossa nova. There is no air conditioning and you look terrible in a jumpsuit. Your cellmate has a face tattoo. You don't know if you will ever see your husband or your daughter again. You wonder how you ended up here.

You are walking through the park carrying seventeen dog leashes. In the distance, you see a pack of dogs that you are responsible for. Half of them are sniffing each other's butts and the other half are fighting. One dog is fighting while having its butt sniffed. You stop, put a plastic bag on your hand, and pick up warm poop. You add it to the large collection of plastic bags containing dog poop that you are carrying. There is no trash can in sight. It is raining. You wonder how you ended up here.

The venomous green juice tastes of grass cuttings, salt, cucumber, algae, and manure.

It stays inside you for seventeen minutes before you have to run to the bathroom to expel it.

┄┄⟩ Turn to 128.

You attach the topless photo to a message to Hot Russell, press send, and your body is immediately filled with an intense burning sensation that could be lust, shame, or the beginnings of a urinary tract infection.

You hear the buzz as the message arrives on Hot Russell's phone, and then, much louder, his gasp, which you hope is not of horror.

"Sorry, did I misjudge the moment?" you whisper.

Hot Russell stares at you. He is blushing.

"What are the two of you playing at?" says your boss.

Hot Russell opens and closes his mouth but no sound comes out.

·····⟩ To distract your boss by telling her that this meeting is a complete waste of time, turn to 4.

·····⟩ To put the blame on Hot Russell, turn to 85.

This is the most exciting, spontaneous, and risky thing you've ever done. (The second most exciting, spontaneous, and risky thing you've ever done was stealing some mascara from Walgreens when you were fourteen.) The sex itself is not very good, however, because you are wedged up against the basin and it's digging into your lower back, which has been flaring up again, ever since your daughter's school field day, when you got too competitive in the three-legged race.

Your daughter. Now you are remembering that you are married, and starting to feel guilty.

After the sex is over, you thank Hot Russell politely and wonder what the hell to do.

·····⫶ To tell your husband what happened, turn to 54.

·····⫶ To keep it to yourself, turn to 50.

You go up to an airport official.

"Hello," you say. "I'm supposed to be flying to Brazil but I've changed my mind. How do I get out of this security area?"

"First we need to get your luggage off the plane," she says.

"I don't have any luggage," you say.

"All you have with you is that small handbag?"

"It was a spur-of-the-moment thing."

"When did you book your ticket?"

"About two hours ago."

"And you just . . . changed your mind."

"That's right."

"One moment."

The airport official steps to one side and speaks into a walkie-talkie.

"OK, come with me."

You think that the airport official is going to take you to some special exit, but in fact she leads you to a small windowless room with two police officers in it. She leaves you there and locks the door behind her.

You have been flagged as acting suspiciously and now you are going to be interrogated. You need to prove that you are not a terrorist, but the only way to do that is to explain to two unsympathetic police officers why your life is a humiliating wreck.

⋯⋯⟩ To tell the police officers the truth, turn to 139.

⋯⋯⟩ To let them believe you are a terrorist, turn to 102.

You refuse to get a motorcycle because you value your internal organs. Your dad offers you a ride home on his new motorcycle but you refuse, also because you value your internal organs. You wave goodbye to him and wonder whether you will ever see him alive again, and then you catch the bus home.

Two hours later you are still sitting on the stationary bus in traffic while happy, debonair people in sexy leather clothes zoom past your window on motorcycles. Have you always been this boring and cautious? What about that time you went skinny-dipping? And that time you ate undercooked chicken?

You inhale the traffic fumes as a small boy repeatedly rings the bell for the next stop and you wonder how you ended up here.

You are on a plane to Brazil! This seems like a great idea and not at all like something a fleeing bank robber or serial killer would do. Because you got a last-minute ticket, you have a lousy seat, between a very little, very old lady and a man with multiple piercings who smells of wheat. It's a long flight to Brazil. Very long.

> ┈┈▷ To watch in-flight entertainment, turn to 39.

> ┈┈▷ To talk to the very little, very old lady, turn to 91.

> ┈┈▷ To talk to the man with the piercings, turn to 2.

You go on the Holistic Emotional Purge retreat, which is being held in a conference center in an industrial park. Your welcome package informs you that this location's combination of city and nature "symbolically balances the yin and yang in all of us." There are about sixty people here. Fifty-nine of them look like Gwyneth Paltrow and the other one is you. A willowy man with a sarong and a man bun leads everyone in an opening meditation in which he invites each person to make a sound representing their current emotional state. There is a lot of sobbing, screaming, and growling. You manage a small, confused whimper.

After the meditation you have a range of options.

⋯⋯⟫ For yoga, turn to 13.

⋯⋯⟫ For a more dynamic meditation, turn to 140.

⋯⋯⟫ For wellness and nutrition advice, turn to 146.

"People come here to have sex, not drink beer," you explain to the tourist. "My husband is over there with—actually, I'd rather not look. But that's what we came here for. It seemed like a good idea at the time. I could have sex with you if you like."

"Sex?" says the tourist. "In a bar?"

He looks very doubtful. You don't blame him. There probably isn't a chapter in the guidebook about this.

"We don't have to have actual sex," you say. You notice that you feel quite relieved. "We could just fool around a bit. Or you could look at my boobs. Or I could spank you."

"Spank? I don't think I know this word . . ."

"It's, um. I hit you. On the bottom."

You mime it. The tourist's face lights up.

"Ah, yes! I hear of this thing! Very American! Very traditional!"

He is very happy now. He hands you the guidebook and bends over his chair.

You are in a swingers bar spanking a tourist using a copy of the *Lonely Planet* guide to the United States. You wonder how you ended up here.

"I read an article on Facebook about polyamory," you tell your husband.

"Isn't that what young people call sleeping around?" says your husband.

"Yes," you say, "but it's ethical. We respect each other and talk about our feelings."

Your husband looks doubtful.

"We don't have to do the talking about our feelings part," you reassure him.

"Well, OK," says your husband, "if you think this is a good idea. Do you already have someone in mind?"

The thought of Hot Russell enters your brain.

⋯⋯⟩ To mention Hot Russell, turn to 150.

⋯⋯⟩ To tell your husband that you have nobody in particular in mind, turn to 53.

Are you too picky, you wonder, as the next image appears: SKULLTHRAX. Skullthrax has huge, frizzy black hair and an enormous beard, and is wearing a T-shirt featuring a decapitated Virgin Mary and the slogan MADONNA WHORE. Every inch of visible skin is covered in tattoos other than his face, which has been painted with fake (you hope) blood. All subsequent pictures are of his guitars.

⋯⋯> Swipe left (no)? Turn to 19.

⋯⋯> Swipe right (yes)? Turn to 55.

You watch three films. All of them have Jennifer Aniston in them. They are all terrible. You still have over five hours of the flight left.

┈┈▷ To talk to the very little, very old lady, turn to 91.

┈┈▷ To talk to the man with the piercings, turn to 2.

Home! Thank goodness. Yes, the entire place needs tidying, and a complete renovation because you haven't touched it since you moved in and you have to use a plunger on the shower drain every time you wash your hair, but nobody here is talking about sales strategies, and that makes you so happy you could weep.

Your husband is in the unmodernized kitchen drinking unmodernized tea from an unmodernized mug. You are so relieved to see him that you are filled with love that obliterates everything else that has happened so far today, as well as his receding hairline, his paunch, his mother, his habit of playing stupid computer games late at night, and the way that when he sleeps on his back it sounds like someone is driving a combine harvester through your bedroom. You were so right to marry him and you should totally delete all of those text messages with your friends where you repeatedly say the exact opposite.

You take the mug out of your husband's hand and lead him into the bedroom.

You have sex. It is like all the other times you have sex.

You lie in your husband's arms. This is exactly as it should be, you think. Everything the way that it always is, and has been for years.

"Do you think our relationship has become a bit boring?" says your husband.

"Oh my god, yes," you say.

"Yeah, me too," says your husband. You feel a little insulted. "I wonder if there is any way we could spice things up?" he adds.

⋯⋯⋗ To suggest opening the relationship, turn to 37.

⋯⋯⋗ To suggest renovating the kitchen, turn to 73.

You rush off to get dressed and call an ambulance but the locker you left your clothes and phone in won't open. Your husband calls the ambulance and stays behind to rescue your possessions while you accompany Hot Russell to the hospital.

At the hospital, someone gives you a dressing gown to wear over your lingerie. Hot Russell is taken to a ward. He is not so hot right now, in a hospital gown and an oxygen mask. What you can see of his skin resembles bright pink bubble wrap. He has an IV in his arm and he is unconscious.

You answer questions from a nurse.

"What is the nature of your relationship with the patient?"

"He's a colleague from work."

"And how did the allergic reaction occur?"

"He was wearing a latex outfit."

"An outfit that also covered his face?"

"That's right."

"And where did the incident take place?"

"At a bar called Mr. and Mrs. and Mr."

Suddenly a woman rushes into the room and runs up to Hot Russell's bedside.

"Who are you?" says the nurse.

"I'm his wife," says the woman. Then she notices you. "Who are *you*?" she says.

⸱⸱⸱⸱⸳ To tell the truth, turn to 65.

⸱⸱⸱⸱⸳ To lie, turn to 134.

"Hello," you say to the tourist. "Are you OK?"

"Is it traditional in the United States that everyone sits in their underwear in a bar?"

"This is a sex bar," you explain.

"Sex bar? In the guide, it says it is a traditional pub."

The tourist shows you the relevant page of the *Lonely Planet*. You examine the book.

"This book is from twenty years ago. I think this place is under new management."

The tourist looks at you quizzically.

"It is not really a pub," you say.

"Also, the beer is very bad," says the tourist.

He doesn't seem to be having a very good time.

⌁⋯⋯⋗ To offer to have sex with the tourist, turn to 36.

⌁⋯⋯⋗ To get the tourist out of there, turn to 77.

You decide to sell the house and move to the country. It will be good for everyone, you say: a fresh start! Yes, your daughter will have to leave behind all her friends and move schools and, yes, your husband will have a ninety-minute commute, and, yes, you have literally no idea what kind of job you will do, and, yes, the value of your property is much lower than it was before you reduced it to a construction site, but think of the positives: nature, clean air, peace and quiet, and you can move into a place where somebody else has already renovated the kitchen.

·······⋯⋗ Turn to 99.

You download an app onto your phone. Now you are learning Swedish. You have never been to Sweden nor do you have any particular desire to go. Swedish is of no use in your career. You have no real interest in Swedish art or culture. You only know one Swedish person, Annika the babysitter, and she speaks better English than you do. Yet somehow, the entire fate of your marriage now rests on you learning to speak Swedish. And so you learn. *Du undrar hur du hamnade här.*

"Hey," you say, "I'm sorry. I've changed my mind. Could you drop me at the corner?"

"But I thought you wanted to do an all-night *Fortnite* marathon?"

You say thanks but no and kiss him on the cheek and get out of the car.

The Uber drives away. You call another one on your phone. Then you wait. You notice that there are quite a few other women waiting for Ubers on this street.

Perhaps inevitably, it starts to rain, hard. The street is dimly lit and it's difficult to make out the license plates of the cars. Cars keep approaching and slowing down, and you lean over and squint into them, as do the other women, trying to figure out whether this driver matches the photo on your phone.

Eventually a car pulls over that you are pretty sure is driven by Yussef and you are just trying to read the number on the license plate to be sure, when the driver gets out and arrests you for soliciting. He is not Yussef.

⤑ Turn to 79.

Oh my god. The next picture is your husband. Your ex-husband, you should say. He is using a photo from your wedding and he has cropped you out of it. How come he's already dating? What if he's seen that you're already dating? And if he's seen your profile, did he swipe yes or swipe no?

Your immediate impulse is to delete the app, but you hesitate. If you swipe yes on your ex-husband, you will find out whether he swiped yes on you.

⋯⋯⟩ To delete the app, turn to 69.

⋯⋯⟩ To swipe yes on your ex-husband, turn to 47.

It's a match! A match with your husband! Your ex-husband! He swiped right on you! You are both flattered and relieved. You send him a jokey message pretending to be a stranger who doesn't know him, and he sends you a similar jokey message back. You text back and forth pretending to flirt and to fall in love with each other. You haven't had this much fun with your (ex-)husband in years. This goes on for weeks. When you see him in person to hand your daughter back and forth, you both pretend that this text communication does not exist. It's incredibly exciting. You desperately want to have sex with your (ex-)husband and you are thrilled when he finally suggests meeting up in person. You spend ages inventing a slutty outfit that your alter ego would wear and you book a hotel room near the bar that he has suggested. An hour before the date, you get a message saying that your (ex-)husband is trapped in Dubai and can you wire him $800 for a plane ticket. You saw your (ex-)husband this morning when he came over to the house to pick up his mail. Your (ex-)husband is not trapped in Dubai. You have been catfished by someone who stole your (ex-)husband's identity on the internet. As you consider the fact that your relationship with the scammer was arguably better than the one you had with your (ex-)husband, you wonder how you ended up here.

You follow the man in the latex fetish suit into a private room, and another man comes in with you.

"Hang on," you say, "I'm not sure I'm up for—"

The second man gets out a camera and starts filming.

"Wait, no—I'm definitely not OK with—"

Meanwhile latex-fetish-suit-man has unzipped his head. You stare at him. He really does look familiar. And then suddenly you know where you've seen him before.

"Were you on that British reality show *Infidelity Island*?" you say.

"Yes! I'm Cheeky Jules! And now I'm expanding my brand as the popular face of nonmonogamy to the US!" He waves at the guy who is filming.

"Great, but I don't want to—"

"This is livestreaming, by the way. Hello, everyone!"

"What the hell? No!"

You lunge at the guy with the camera, but Cheeky Jules grabs you and pulls you back. You fight with Cheeky Jules to try to get the camera. Every time you nearly get away from him and get hold of the camera, Cheeky Jules says, "Now, that's cheeky!"

"That's a really annoying catchphrase!" you yell at Cheeky Jules.

Finally you manage to get the camera off the other guy, but the footage has already been broadcast. There's not much you can do about it so you give the camera back.

⋯⋯⟩ Turn to 88.

You're not pregnant. You are devastated by the news. But you have to admit that a small part of you is relieved that you are not going to have to go through the terrible twos all over again, this time on your own.

Your choices now are straightforward: Try again or move on?

┈┈⟩ To try again, turn to 20.

┈┈⟩ To move on, turn to 14.

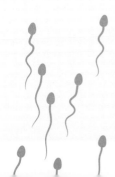

You go back into the meeting, which is as boring as it ever was, only now you can feel waves of shame radiating off you, which you are sure everybody there can sense, not least because Hot Russell keeps glancing at you and smirking. He is not that hot, actually, now you think of it. And then you know that you are really feeling guilty because Hot Russell *is* definitely that hot; you showed his LinkedIn profile to a bunch of your friends after a particular boozy "let's drink wine every time someone cries on *The Bachelor*" night and they all agreed. If he wasn't that hot, why would you call him Hot Russell? The remorse is making you lose your mind, and your boss droning on about search engine optimization is not helping at all, and what the hell does SEO have to do with the sales strategy anyway? You refuse to listen to find out.

You are never going to make it to the end of the meeting.

⸱⸱⸱⸱⸱▷ To tell your boss that this meeting is a complete waste of time, turn to 4.

⸱⸱⸱⸱⸱▷ To run away from your office and down the street, turn to 141.

When your contractors finally come back from the other house they are working on, they tell you that you have dry rot and condensation and that the beams holding up the floor are riddled with termites and need to be replaced. They add that these problems go beyond the kitchen to the entire house, and by the way have you noticed that the electrical wiring was installed illegally and is extremely dangerous?

This gives you an idea.

⋯⋯⟩ To burn down your house, turn to 145.

⋯⋯⟩ To resist the powerful urge to burn down your house, turn to 43.

Your dad and the salesperson ride off together on a motorcycle, the salesperson in front, your dad clinging on behind. You are terrified, and yet you find that you also feel proud of him for being so brave in this new phase of his life. It reminds you of your daughter's first day at school.

When they get back, your dad is completely exhilarated. "You should try it!" he says, handing you his helmet. You protest, but he's in earnest, so eventually you agree and climb on behind the salesperson.

It is amazing. Zooming through the streets, you feel fully alive for the first time in ages. Maybe you should buy a motorcycle!

⋯⋯⟫ To buy a motorcycle, turn to 74.

⋯⋯⟫ To come to your senses and not buy a motorcycle, turn to 33.

"No," you say, "but apparently there are whole communities of people who do it together, and are very happy, and probably vegan."

Your husband sits up in bed in excitement.

"I've been meaning to try Veganuary! Plus Dinesh on my office softball team said that he read about a swingers club near here. He saw it in an in-flight magazine, but his wife wouldn't let him go. We could go there!"

⋯⋯⟩ To point out to your husband that he would never be able to endure life without cheese, turn to 59.

⋯⋯⟩ To agree to the swingers night, turn to 82.

You find a quiet spot in the corner of the office, between the untouched pile of free company newsletters and the soup and coffee machine that makes all the coffee taste like soup and the soup taste like sad water. You take a deep breath and phone your husband.

"What is it?" he says. "You never call me at work. Are you sick? Did we forget a parents' evening? Did my mother call you for computer advice again?"

"I've got something to tell you," you say, and you explain what happened. You are very careful not to refer to Hot Russell as "Hot Russell."

There is a long silence. You are beginning to wonder if the signal has dropped when he says, "Is this the end?"

Is it?

┈┈┈> To divorce your husband, turn to page 143.

┈┈┈> To find a way to save your marriage, turn to 12.

It's a match! Skullthrax invites you to a death-metal gig. He sends you a ticket and says that he'll meet you inside. When you get in, the band is already playing. It sounds like you are having a migraine on a construction site in hell. You can't find Skullthrax anywhere. It takes you a while to realize that he is in the band on the stage. He's actually pretty good at the guitar, but you're less keen on the way he bites into dead rats and drinks their blood.

Afterward you have a drink at the bar. Skullthrax tells you that his day job is in insurance. He shows genuine interest in your work and your daughter. You are surprised to find that you like him, but when he tries to kiss you, you remember the rats. He goes to brush his teeth but you don't think that will help. While you are waiting for him to come back, somebody in the next band starts throwing pig entrails into the audience. Some of it lands in your drink. You decide that this is not your scene.

⤏ To try again for another match, turn to 19.

⤏ To delete the app, turn to 69.

Sex has changed since you last dated. This guy is completely hairless from the neck down, like one of those anti-allergy cats. He is very vigorous, and there is a lot of activity involving your bottom. At one point he strangles you. You say no thanks and he apologizes politely and lets go of your neck but he looks a bit surprised that you would object. If you are going to be single now, you are going to need to watch a lot more pornography as a research aid.

As soon as the sex is over, he opens three different social media sites and starts posting things. You look over his shoulder in case he is writing about you but all you see is a gif of someone in a mobility scooter knocking over some cans. It could be a metaphor for something but you don't know what.

You have breakfast together. His kitchen looks like the site of a science experiment gone badly wrong and gives you terrifying flashbacks to your college days. You accept some toast but turn down coffee on the grounds that there is something growing in the milk.

He asks whether you'd like to see him again.

⋯⋯⟩ You would! Turn to 23.

⋯⋯⟩ No thanks! Turn to 75.

You snort. You have only ever seen people do this on TV and you are disappointed that a rolled-up $50 bill is not involved. The disappointment doesn't last, though, because this is AMAZING. You feel like the best-looking, most interesting person in the room. You dance like that person too. Or at least you think you do. You also talk like that person, and the young stranger who gave you the drugs goes away quite quickly after that, but you don't care. This is the greatest experience of your life and you are totally doing this again.

······⟩ Turn to 111.

You continue going to couples therapy. You go once a week for more than six months. It sort of, for lack of a better word, works.

You are semi-happily married to a pretty normal guy who you basically love. Your daughter is mostly great though often very annoying, and your job is OK. Your house could be better but it could be worse. You have some decent friends and your parents are essentially tolerable. Your life is more or less fine. You wonder how you ended up here.

You remind your husband at great length of his attachment to eating cheese, until eventually he concedes, with tears in his eyes, that Veganuary would not be a good idea. This discussion of dairy products brings the conversation back around to the kitchen, and you both agree that, actually, home renovations are bound to be a less dangerous path to revitalizing your marriage than sleeping with other people, even if the DIY catastrophe that ended your first long-term relationship suggests otherwise.

······⟩ Turn to 73.

The dating app is exactly the way you remember it from all the times you drunkenly wrestled the phone out of a single friend's hands and started right-swiping on really unattractive people for a laugh. You now realize that wasn't funny at all. You upload some flattering, recent (from within the last ten years) pictures of yourself and agonize over the two lines of text that will imply that while you are looking for true love, you would also be up for some casual hookups, but that you are even pickier about who you hook up with for fun than you are about who you have true love with. Then you start swiping.

The first guy to come up is MARTYN. The photo was taken by the sea. Martyn is sunburned and is holding up a large fish. He and the fish both have the same underbite.

······⋙ Swipe left for no—turn to 97.

······⋙ Swipe right for yes—turn to 103.

61

Apologize? Who are you kidding?

┄┄┄⟩ Turn to 89.

The fire department notices suspicious activity, and the fire is traced back to a vodka bottle that your husband identifies as a gift that you were given by a friend from Moscow who stayed with you for a week for a symposium on mental health and impulse control in perimenopausal women.

You are arrested for arson. You plead guilty and break down in court, citing the names of the 104 color swatches you tried on your kitchen in mitigation. The judge tells you that she has also recently been redoing her kitchen and sentences you to community service.

As you meet with a group of your fellow criminals, put on a fluorescent vest, and spend your day scrubbing pee and graffiti from the underpass beneath the beltway, you wonder how you ended up here.

You call up your best single friend. This is going to be amazing, you think, as the phone rings. Two girls out on the town! Hooking up with guys! Getting laid! Wild! Crazy! Maybe you can get some pills! You don't know what pills actually are (Speed? Ecstasy? Aspirin?) but you've heard people talking about them and you want some. Anyway, your friend will know! She's single!

Your best single friend answers the phone. "Hey, it's great that you called," she says. "Actually, I could really use a favor. Can you come with me to the IVF clinic?"

"The IVF clinic?"

"Yes, I finally decided I want to have a baby on my own. It's now or never, you know? But I would really love to have a friend there with me for the first appointment, I'm a bit nervous."

"So . . . you don't want to go clubbing?"

"Clubbing? I haven't been clubbing for fifteen years."

You should probably talk to your best single friend more often.

·····⋗ To go with your friend to the IVF clinic, turn to 78.

·····⋗ To go clubbing by yourself, turn to 124.

"I'm sorry, Russell," you say, "this has all been a terrible misunderstanding. I realize that you might have gotten the wrong idea from me sending you that picture of my boobs, but I forgot that I am incapable of having sex in a restroom, after an unfortunate incident on a long-haul flight when I was nineteen that led to an emergency landing and three days' incarceration in an airport jail, where the reading material was very limited. Please don't take it personally, as you are extremely hot."

Russell shakes your hand like a grown-up, and goes back into the meeting. You think he might be holding back tears but you're not sure. You consider giving him a tissue but that would mean following him back into the meeting and you can't face it. You can't break his heart by flaunting yourself in front of him, and also the meeting was really boring.

┈┈⟫ To go home, turn to 40.

┈┈⟫ To run away from your office down the street, turn to 141.

"Actually . . . I'm the one who brought him to the hospital," you tell Mrs. Hot Russell, hoping to put the most positive spin on it. (Mrs. Hot Russell is also quite hot, you notice.)

"You mean, you were the one he was cheating on me with in the swingers bar?" says Mrs. Hot Russell.

"We didn't do anything," you say.

"Only because he nearly died," says Mrs. Hot Russell.

"No, actually—" you begin, but it's too late. Mrs. Hot Russell leaps on you and starts to slap and kick you while emitting the yips and growls of a Yorkshire terrier that has been trodden on.

⋯⋯⋗ Turn to 66.

You are in a hospital bed suffering from swinging-related injuries. You are covered with cuts and bruises from Hot Russell's angry wife, and the underwiring of your slutty bra got detached in the fight and cut open your armpit, requiring stitches. (Both you and the bra.) You wonder how to come up with a convincing story for the person in the next bed about how you ended up here.

"Do you come here often?" says the man in the head-to-toe latex fetish suit.

Half of you can't believe that people still use that line, while the other half wonders whether his voice sounds familiar. Well, that's not entirely true, because seven-eighths of you is freaking out about being in a sticky suburban swingers bar, but in terms of what's available of your attention, it's about fifty/fifty.

"It's my first time," you say.

"Oh, a virgin," says the man in the latex suit.

It amazes you that despite his outfit, the most off-putting thing about him is his conversation.

"Do you want to go to a private room?" he asks through his latex face mask.

You look over at your husband. He has his hand on the corseted woman's breast.

You look at the tourist. He has just ordered "one ale" in an accent you can't place.

To go and talk to the tourist, turn to 42.

To go to a private room with latex man, turn to 11.

To run away to Brazil, turn to 34.

You arrive to pick up your mother and she looks phenomenal, like she's been in one of those "stylish at every age" features in a fashion magazine.

"You should think about updating your wardrobe," she says when she sees your outfit. "It's not the '90s anymore."

"I can't afford to do that!"

"Nonsense! Everything I'm wearing cost under $40 and came from H&M and Target."

When you shop at H&M and Target you end up looking like you covered yourself in glue and rolled around in a final call sale.

In the nightclub queue, four different people come over and ask your mother whether she is Helen Mirren. The bouncers spot her and usher her to the front of the line. They look critically at you but she explains that you are with her and so they reluctantly let you in.

It's EDM night. The music is very loud but your mother has come equipped with earplugs (one pair, for herself) and is soon dancing with enthusiasm.

"It's got a good beat!" she says.

She is soon surrounded by endless people who want to dance with her. They get between you and her, and gradually you find yourself being moved farther and farther away until you end up at the periphery of the dance floor with a teenage boy who looks like he is about to vomit and a girl in her twenties who can't stop crying, probably related to the couple making out a few steps away. Clubbing used to be more fun, you think.

By 3 a.m. you are exhausted and desperate to go home but your mother trots past you on the way back from the restroom looking as fresh as the moment she arrived, and says, "This is great!" before disappearing back into the crowd. You order yet another hard seltzer in a can and you wonder how you ended up here.

You delete the app. Years pass. You never date anybody ever again and you die alone. As you lie on your deathbed, lonely and unloved, you wonder how you ended up here.

The very little, very old lady is delighted to show you her hospitality. She talks animatedly about all the delicious food she is going to cook for you. It is basically all going to be meat. You decide not to mention that you have been trying to eat less meat lately, for environmental reasons largely canceled out by this unnecessary flight to Brazil.

You don't have any luggage but you wait for her at the baggage claim, where she picks up an insane number of suitcases. She piles them so high on the trolley that there is no way she can see her way forward, let alone push the trolley. "Could you help me with this?" she asks.

·····⟫ To help the very little, very old lady with her luggage, turn to 129.

·····⟫ To refuse to help the very little, very old lady with her luggage, turn to 16.

You can't get a recommendation for a place to get cosmetic procedures because nobody you know has ever admitted to having them and if you asked it would suggest that you thought that they had. In the end, you use one that you find on Groupon. There's a discount for multiple procedures so you have slightly more done than you might otherwise have gone for, but the practitioner assures you that it isn't anything too extreme, just a bit of smoothing and plumping to help you regain a youthful glow.

What you end up with is a face that resembles what would happen if the Stay Puft Marshmallow Man had all his wisdom teeth pulled.

You consider your options—Wear a veil? Wrap your entire face in bandages? Stay alone in a darkened room until it eventually subsides?—before deciding to just brazen it out.

Each time someone you meet flinches, averts their eyes, and babbles incoherently until the shock wears off, you wonder how you ended up here.

Inner transformation. That's exactly what you need. You remember some information you were given at work about a Holistic Emotional Purge weekend for people suffering from burnout, and decide that it's just the thing.

·····⟩ Turn to 35.

Renovate the kitchen! It's a great idea! How hard can it be? You only need new paint, new tiles, new cabinets, new counters, new floor tiles, an exhaust fan that actually works, maybe change the layout, move all the plumbing around, finally take care of those drains, and the window frames are looking a bit rotten and maybe should be replaced, and in fact should you consider an extension on the side of the house?

"This will be a fun project we can do together!" you tell your husband.

You give him some paint swatches to look at. He goes so pale that he matches Mouse's Footprint, or possibly First Gray Hair, or Lint. They are quite similar.

"Why don't you pick the one that you want?" he says.

"I'm not going to do this all myself!" you say.

Or are you? Toss a coin!

⋯⋯⋗ If you get heads, turn to 107.

⋯⋯⋗ If you get tails, turn to 115.

You buy a motorcycle. It is ridiculously expensive, but you remind yourself of all the money you've saved in your life by never having been a smoker. You could probably afford two motorcycles by now! (You will not test this theory by actually doing the math.)

You own a motorcycle! An actual, honest-to-god motorcycle! You are born to be wild! Or at least to weave through traffic jams. You look young and cool—with the helmet on, nobody can see your wrinkles—except that you drive as badly as a teenage pizza delivery boy on a moped.

Your dad also buys a motorcycle. He is obviously having some kind of delayed midlife crisis.

You and your dad ride through the streets in convoy, pretty slowly because actually you are both scared of the cars now that the salesperson is not in charge. In the right light, though, you could pass for Hell's Angels. (The right light would be pitch black.) You are a middle-aged woman out riding a motorcycle with your dad. You wonder how you ended up here.

You apologize and say that you can't enter into a relationship with someone who was born after the Spice Girls split up (even the first time), and go home.

Even though you don't want to enter into a relationship with this manchild, you feel emboldened by the fact that you've had sex with someone other than your husband. You decide that the time is right to enter the world of online dating.

·····➤ Turn to 60.

The mindfulness and anger management online workshop consists of a website that plays the soothing sound of gently falling rain while you sit watching your breath and experiencing the full range of your feelings for half an hour. After five minutes, you want to pee. After ten minutes, you think you might die of boredom. After fifteen minutes you are so full of rage you could kill a man with your bare hands. At this rate, by half an hour you will be rampaging through the city like a mindful Godzilla, staying present with your exhale while you knock down buildings and piss on cars.

⤳ To go back to Human Resources and ask to go on the wellness retreat instead, turn to 35.

⤳ To give up and surf Twitter, turn to 122.

You take the tourist over to your husband. "We need to get this guy out of here. He's here by mistake. He just wants to drink beer."

"I want to learn American traditions," says the tourist.

"I've got some good brews at home, actually," says your husband.

"We can drink beer!" says the tourist with a huge smile.

The three of you get dressed and go home. Your husband stays up late drinking beer with the tourist. They hit it off like crazy, and your husband invites the tourist to stay.

"Traditional American hospitality!" says the tourist.

You can't bring yourself to ask the tourist when he is leaving, and so he just stays.

You now have a tourist who you met in a swingers bar living in your house. Your daughter is teaching him English. Your husband keeps buying him beer. You have no idea if he will ever go home. You wonder how he ended up here.

You go with your best single friend to her appointment at the clinic. The doctor is extremely short and very ugly and he makes a lot of leering comments that at first you don't understand, until you realize that he's assuming that you and your friend are a lesbian couple. You consider not correcting him in case he takes your heterosexuality as a come-on, but you draw the line when he starts explaining to you how to inject hormones into your friend's backside. Having clarified the situation, you stop listening, because you are afraid of needles. Instead, you look around the walls. The room is covered with pictures of babies. You know that it's meant as encouragement but it's also pretty tactless. The babies are so cute, it will just make people want them even more. You start reminiscing about how adorable your daughter was at that age, forgetting all the screaming, shitting, puking, the agonizing breastfeeding, the six hours it took to leave the house, the endless laundry, the relentless boredom, and the whole bit where she ripped your vagina to pieces being born.

You begin to feel overwhelmed with desire for another baby. You know it's completely irrational, and yet the urge to hold your very own, brand-new, tiny little child in your arms gets stronger and stronger. And this might be your last chance. . . .

Should you have another baby?

⋯⋯⟫ Yes! Turn to 149.

⋯⋯⟫ No! Turn to 94.

You are at the police station in a holding cell full of prostitutes. Everyone is discussing *The Great British Baking Show*. You nearly call your husband to come and bail you out but then you remember that you are divorced so you have to call your mother instead. She is not impressed. It reminds you of the time you were caught smoking at school, except this time the other girls who are also in trouble have marginally longer skirts. My god, the things you wore back then. You make a mental note to double-check the length of all your daughter's skirts, and you wonder how you ended up here.

"You're right to do this, Mom," you say. "You're still young . . . at heart. Why not enjoy your life before it's too late?"

"That's what I was hoping you'd say," says your mother. "Because I need your help embracing the wild woman within. What do you think I should do to celebrate being single again?"

⋯⋯⟩ To help your mother set up an online dating profile, turn to 137.

⋯⋯⟩ To take your mother to a nightclub, turn to 68.

So. Shave your head, or Botox and fillers?

┈┈╌> Shave your head: 9.

┈┈╌> Botox and fillers: 71.

You look up on the internet what to wear to a swingers night, but the search results are so terrifying that you resort to your Little Black Dress for All Occasions, which has already served you well at the office Christmas party, your great-aunt's funeral, and that time you had to give evidence in a court hearing after witnessing a traffic accident. Your husband wears his best jeans and a plain shirt. It was either that or his work suit. You are much more worried about his underwear. You have some good slutty stuff that you bought on a bachelorette weekend but never wear because it itches, but all of his underpants have cartoon characters on them. At the last minute, you remember his plain navy Speedos. Maybe it will be dark enough that nobody will notice.

⋯⋯⋗ If your husband wears his Bugs Bunny underpants, turn to 105.

⋯⋯⋗ If he wears the Speedos, turn to 105 anyway. There is no getting out of this.

You dig around in your bag and find a tissue for the junior account executive. She blows her nose. Everyone is grateful.

The meeting has now been going on for nineteen and a half minutes.

⋯⋯> If you want to write a note to Hot Russell, turn to 131.

⋯⋯> If you want to tell your boss that this meeting is a complete waste of time, turn to 4.

Desire to run screaming from the room

There are no desks or chairs in Human Resources, just a very young barefoot man sitting cross-legged on a floor cushion, with another cushion in front of him. Is he Generation Z? Is he younger than Gen Z? What is younger than Gen Z? A fetus?

You lower yourself to the cushion.

"Tea?" he says. "It's ylang-ylang, nettle, and stinkweed. Very cleansing. No? So tell me, what inspired you to come today?"

You explain your situation.

"Wow," he says. "That's powerful stuff. I empathize, though obviously I would never have done what you did. What I sense is a lack of balance in your life. Do you have any experience with wellness?"

"I do yoga," you say, which is an exaggeration.

"Really? I would never have guessed it, from how you're sitting. Anyway, I have a couple of recommendations that might help you. I can sign you up for a Holistic Emotional Purge retreat this weekend, or I can offer some online tutorials in mindfulness and anger management."

⋯⋯⋗ To go on the wellness retreat, turn to 35.

⋯⋯⋗ To take the online course, turn to 76.

"I just asked Russell for the sales figures from this quarter's report, and he was completely unprepared," you tell your boss.

"Is that right, Russell?" says your boss.

Toss a coin!

┈┈▷ If you get heads, turn to 5.

┈┈▷ If you get tails, turn to 15.

Next up for consideration is NIGHT TIGER. Night Tiger is shirtless and stares, sultry, into the bathroom mirror as he holds up his phone to take the photo. The mirror is covered in flecks of toothpaste or, possibly, Night Tiger is. His caption reads: I AM NIGHT TIGER I SHOW U GOOD TIME ALL NIGHT GAURUNTEED. NIGHT TIGER MAKE U HAPPY I PROMISS. CHOSE NIGHT TIGER.

·····⟩ Swipe left for no—turn to 46.

·····⟩ Swipe right for yes—turn to 148.

You chicken out.

"I'm not really a druggy person," you tell the shaman, overlooking your massive yet socially acceptable wine habit.

"OK. Want to watch?" says the shaman.

"Sure!" you say.

It turns out mid-ceremony that you don't actually want to watch, listen, or smell as the mass purging (both ends in some cases) gets underway.

"I'm just going to go, um—" you start to say to the shaman, but he's as wasted as anyone and he's not listening.

You walk away, pretty quickly. Arguably you are running. You are running through the jungle in Brazil, at night.

You stop running.

You are alone and completely lost in the jungle in Brazil, at night.

You wonder how you ended up here. Wherever here is. Where is here?

The clip of you wrestling with Cheeky Jules goes viral. You are now internet famous. Wherever you go, people call out to you, "Wrestle the latex man," "Now, that's cheeky!" and "That's a really annoying catchphrase!," which is, indeed, a really annoying catchphrase. Nevertheless, you are hired to appear on a comedy game show on live TV, where your job is to shout "That's a really annoying catchphrase!" when comedians use their catchphrases. The job is ridiculous but the money is good. As you sit under the hot studio lights waiting for your cue, you wonder how you ended up here.

That is SO UNFAIR, you text your husband. *You LITERALLY told me that it is your FANTASY that I would text you my BOOBS in a CLIENT MEETING. Is it MY fault YOU were using your PERSONAL laptop for WORK?!* (You are using a lot of all caps because you know that he hates it.)

The reply comes: *I also told you that I have a fantasy about having sex on the field at Yankee Stadium, but I don't actually want to do that because (a) I would get arrested and (b) I don't want my bare ass on SportsCenter. There is a difference between fantasy and reality, and PS, stop using all caps, I hate it.*

I KNOW there is a difference between FANTASY and REALITY. I have, IN REALITY, been married to YOU long enough to be VERY clear about THAT.

If you have been married to me for long enough, maybe we should get a divorce! PS YOUR USE OF ALL CAPS DOESN'T EVEN MAKE SENSE.

Maybe you SHOULD get a divorce. (All caps is invading your thinking now.) Or maybe you just need time to cool off.

┈┈╌➢ To take some space and go to your parents' place, turn to 104.

┈┈╌➢ To make an appointment with a divorce lawyer, turn to 143.

You are in an Uber with a total stranger from a nightclub. A cute young total stranger. Your ears are ringing because the club was so loud. You hope that your hearing hasn't been permanently damaged, not least because apparently you have a habit of saying yes to questions you can't hear, and you might end up accidentally married to this person because you don't know that he's proposed. You could learn sign language, but there probably isn't time between now and getting to his place. You know nothing about this guy. You don't even know if you're going to his place for sex or to help him assemble IKEA furniture. (It's probably sex.) Is this really a good idea?

⋯⋯⋯⟩ To continue on to the cute young total stranger's apartment, turn to 92.

⋯⋯⋯⟩ To get out of the car, turn to 45.

The very little, very old lady is only too happy to talk to you. She is Brazilian and on her way back from visiting her daughter, who is working as a dental technician in Rhode Island. She gets out her phone and starts showing you pictures of her children. And of her grandchildren. And of her one beloved great-grandson. And of her brothers and sisters. And of her nieces and nephews. And of her grandnieces and grandnephews. And of some random people she met in Rhode Island. It is a *really* long flight to Brazil.

As the flight comes in to land, she asks you whether you have somewhere to stay, and if not, would you like to come and stay with her?

┅┅⊱ To go and stay with the very little, very old lady, turn to 70.

┅┅⊱ To take your chances on your own in Rio, turn to 151.

You are kissing the cute young stranger on his couch. He probably did tell you his name at some point in the club but you couldn't hear him and it feels a bit late to ask now. He is very enthusiastic, and you remember having this much energy, a long time ago, before you had your daughter and had to hand over 75 percent of your energy to her. You wonder whether this cute young stranger is closer to her age than to yours. The thought will not go away. When he gets up to go to the bathroom, you look at his driver's license. On the one hand, what you are doing is at least legal. On the other, there's a jar of cumin in your spice rack that is older than he is.

When he comes back in, he asks you what you're humming.

"'Mrs. Robinson.'"

He looks at you blankly.

"Simon and Garfunkel? It's the theme to *The Graduate*? Anne Bancroft? Dustin Hoffman?"

He has no idea who or what these things are. He probably doesn't even watch films, just gifs and YouTube videos.

The cute young stranger has his hands up your top. Is this sane? Is it even ethical? What about Tilda Swinton, isn't her boyfriend twenty years younger than she is? But Tilda Swinton is a bohemian goddess and her boyfriend has definitely heard of Dustin Hoffman. Would Tilda Swinton sleep with someone who has four half-eaten Cup Noodles on their coffee table?

What would Tilda Swinton do?

┈┈┈⟩ Tilda Swinton would surrender to her desire. Age is irrelevant and so are Cup Noodles. Turn to 56.

┈┈┈⟩ Tilda Swinton would rise above this situation. In fact, she would quite possibly literally levitate out of there. Turn to 101.

You enroll in an evening class. You are now studying physics. It turns out that physics is very hard to understand without math, which you have not studied since high school, and even then you were more interested in reading magazines hidden inside your textbook, so you enroll in another evening class to study mathematics. With homework, you are now studying math and physics every night of the week. All the other students are teenagers making up for flunking out of their high school classes, and spending every break staring at their phones, except for one overwhelmingly upbeat woman who is at least fifteen years older than you and has sad eyes and keeps trying to get you to go to her Seniors Stretch and Supple class and saying, "We oldies have to stick together." Eventually you cave in and go to the Seniors Stretch and Supple class and you keep waiting for someone to tell you that you are too young to be there but they don't and, as you reach down and fail to touch your toes, you wonder how you ended up here.

You close your eyes to block out all the cute baby propaganda on the walls and think about mastitis until the urge to procreate passes. And then you decide to go clubbing by yourself.

······⟫ Turn to 124.

The stockbroker is really helpful. You don't know how you'd sort through all the thousands of different options without her. At her suggestion, you put all your money into a currency called ConCoin. Then you go home.

Three hours later, there is a knock at your front door. It's two nice gentlemen from the FBI. Over coffee, they explain that your company has had all of its assets and private information stolen by a Trojan horse malware that has been traced back to a transaction made from an on-site computer with your log-in. Have you ever heard of something called ConCoin?

The two nice gentlemen from the FBI seize all of your electronic devices and then they seize you. You are taken to an undisclosed location and questioned at length about your links to organized crime and cyberterrorism. Because it is a matter of national security, you are not permitted to know the exact nature of the charges against you, but you are allowed access to a lawyer. The only lawyer you know is the woman who helped you buy your house, and as you wait for her to come to the undisclosed location you wonder how you ended up here.

You go to the motorcycle showroom with your dad. The whole way there, you are trying to talk him out of it.

"Dad," you say, "you are too old for this. You won't be able to wear your progressive lenses with the helmet and you will not be able to see where you are going and you will crash into something."

"Who cares?" says your dad. "We all have to die eventually. Anyway, chicks love motorcycles."

"Dad, you can't say 'chicks' unless you are actually referring to baby chickens."

"Look, the salesman is a chick!"

The salesperson is in fact a burly woman covered in tattoos. You try to get her on your side, but she thinks your dad is cool—the same dad who won't eat pasta because it's foreign—and she gets her phone out and starts showing him pictures of old geezers on Harleys. Your dad and the salesperson have an animated conversation about motorcycles and tattoos and the salesperson asks if she can friend him on Facebook and your dad says he doesn't know what Facebook is.

⋯⋯⟩ To distract your dad by taking him to get a tattoo, which at least won't kill him, turn to 121.

⋯⋯⟩ To give in and let your dad test-ride a motorcycle, turn to 52.

The next option is GUS. It is hard to tell much about Gus because his profile photo is of four men in a badly lit bar. They are all holding up pints of beer. You don't know which of the men Gus is. Maybe they all are. Maybe we are all Gus now.

┈┈> To swipe left (no) on Gus, turn to 38.

┈┈> To swipe right (yes) on Gus, turn to 125.

There are an incredible number of ways to get rich online but once you have eliminated all the illegal and immoral ones, all that are left are dog walking and cryptocurrencies.

⋯⋯⋟ To become a dog walker, turn to 28.

⋯⋯⋟ To invest all your savings in cryptocurrencies, turn to 133.

You are living in a house in the middle of nowhere. If you want a quart of milk, it's a twenty-minute drive. Your husband's commute is supposed to be an hour and a half each way but with traffic it's more like three. Your commute is immaterial because all of your time will now be spent driving your daughter around. The house is cold and drafty, and the garden is full of weeds. You've heard rumors that there are some nice walks around here, but it hasn't stopped raining since you moved. The Wi-Fi is terrible and DoorDash doesn't deliver to your area. Your husband hates you. Your daughter hates you. You have no friends. You sit in your fantastic kitchen and you wonder how you ended up here.

100

The sludge juice tastes of mud, beets, alfalfa, soy, and blood. It stays inside you for fourteen minutes before you have to run to the bathroom to expel it.

┈┈┈▷ Turn to 128.

"I'm sorry," you say, "I make it a policy not to have sex with anyone whose formative *Star Wars* movies were the prequels."

But when you wake up alone in bed the next day, you realize that you feel lonely.

┈┈⟫ To try online dating, turn to 60.

┈┈⟫ To remind yourself that romantic love is not the only form of love, go and visit your parents. Turn to 104.

Obviously it is not ideal, being interrogated for hours in a windowless room about terrorist activities that you have not, in fact, participated in, but at least it's not embarrassing. Eventually, though, they are unable to come up with any evidence linking you to terrorism—obviously—and so they let you go.

┈┈┈⟩ Turn to 123.

It's a match! On your first date with Martyn you go to a fish restaurant—his choice. He talks about fishing a lot. Really a lot. You are telling yourself that it's good for a man to have a hobby when he mentions taking his son fishing. Sensing a possible escape from the fishing talk, you ask him about his son. It turns out that he is married with two kids. He claims to be separated but it emerges that he and his wife still live together, but they haven't had sex for six months, so he considers the relationship over. No, he hasn't told her yet, he doesn't want to upset her. No, she doesn't know that he is dating online.

As you leave the restaurant, Martyn is talking in detail about types of live bait. The last words you hear from him are "fat juicy maggot."

⸱⸱⸱⸱⸱> To try again for another match, turn to 97.

⸱⸱⸱⸱⸱> To delete the app, turn to 69.

Your mother answers the door.

"There you are," she says, sounding annoyed to have been kept waiting, even though she didn't know you were coming. "You look tired. When did you last do your roots? Why do I never see my granddaughter?"

You follow her inside. There are suitcases everywhere.

"Are you going on vacation?" you ask.

"What? Oh, the suitcases! No, your father is moving out."

"*What??*"

"We're getting a divorce."

"*You're* getting a divorce?"

"I've been in his shadow long enough. I may be old, but I'm not dead yet. I want to live!"

Take sides!

······⋗ To take your mother's side, turn to 80.

······⋗ To take your father's side, turn to 116.

The swingers club is down a side street and has an entrance with a velour rope. The woman at the door looks at you long and hard before sighing and unclipping the rope.

"Whatever," she says. "It's a quiet night."

You pay a lot of money and head down a stairwell toward a darkened room where some 1990s house music is playing. You glance inside and immediately realize that you made the wrong decision about your husband's underpants. There is a changing room where you take off your dress and put it in a locker. You tell your husband to remain fully clothed until and unless he is required to go naked. Then you head into the main room.

There are . . . things happening. You take a deep breath.

You both look around for someone who isn't already occupied to strike up a conversation with. Your husband heads over to a redhead in a PVC corset that is giving her chafe marks. There are two men who you could approach.

⋯⋯⟫ To talk to the man in the head-to-toe latex fetish suit, turn to 67.

⋯⋯⟫ To talk to the nervous-looking man in boxer shorts who is sitting in the corner reading a *Lonely Planet* guide to the United States, turn to 42.

A message appears on your screen.

What the hell do you think you're doing? Your message appeared midway through a PowerPoint presentation. Our biggest client and the entire R&D team saw your breasts. Now I've got to go to a meeting with HR to talk about my professionalism.

┈┈▷ To apologize to your husband, turn to 61.

┈┈▷ To tell your husband that it's his own fault, turn to 89.

┈┈▷ To retaliate for your husband's unfair response by sending the topless picture to Hot Russell, turn to 30.

"You're just better at these things than I am," says your husband.

You're not sure, exactly, that you are good at sitting in a pile of rubble, crying on the phone to your builders who have gone to the other house they are working on and given no indication of when they plan to return, while simultaneously searching online for a match for the tiles that you didn't order enough of and that have since been discontinued, and trying to persuade your picky daughter to eat yet another microwave meal for dinner. Also there is no way of telling if your husband is bad at it. When he acknowledges what is happening at all, he insists on referring to it as "your project."

"It's not 'my project,' it's our kitchen," you say.

"I was fine with it as it was," says your husband. This is not true. Your husband has been complaining about the kitchen for over a decade.

·····⋗ To quit, turn to 25.

·····⋗ To persist, turn to 51.

You are now unemployed. What are you going to do? Your family needs two incomes! How are you going to tell your husband that you lost your job for no reason whatsoever other than that you are a total idiot with no impulse control? You are pretty sure that he will not do what you are hoping he will do (give you a massive hug and a slice of cake, or a hug and a massive slice of cake, say that it's OK and you never have to work again, and that you have won the lottery).

You can't go home.

⋯⋯▷ To run as fast as you can away from your office and down the street, turn to 141.

⋯⋯▷ To come up with a plan for securing a new income stream, turn to 17.

⋯⋯▷ To try to get your job back by going to Human Resources and pleading temporary insanity, turn to 84.

You can't let this go.

┈┈⟶ Turn to 6.

"Thanks for the offer," you say, "but I have very delicate nostrils."

He looks around and shoves the Ziploc bag in your hand.

"Seriously, it's very sweet of you but this is a new top and I can't risk getting a nosebleed. It's dry clean only."

Before he can challenge you on who would wear a dry-clean-only top to a nightclub, you feel a hand on your shoulder. You turn around. It is a police officer. He points to the bag in your hand.

"It isn't mine!" you say. "A total stranger just handed it to me! Also I think it might just be bath products."

It makes no difference. You are arrested for possession of drugs. If you had known you were going to get arrested you would have taken the damn drugs, or possibly showered with them, but it's too late now. As you are escorted to a police car waiting outside the club, you wonder how you ended up here.

You bring your daughter to school with a drug hangover coupled with a booze hangover. You are wearing pajamas and Crocs and huge sunglasses that cover almost your entire face. Your daughter walks four paces behind you in the hope that nobody will realize you are together. You are exhausted and you might vomit and you ache all over and your throat feels like sandpaper and there are children everywhere making child noises and they Will. Not. Stop. The mother you hate the most has seen what is visible of your face and is going on and on about Dayquil. You wish for death. You are never doing this again.

······⋙ Turn to 153.

"It's more than just sex," your husband insists. "We have a genuine connection."

"Just because she's Swedish and you've been to IKEA twice does not mean you have a genuine connection! The second time you just sat in the cafeteria eating meatballs while I lifted flat-pack Billy bookshelves onto the cart on my own! I can't believe you're screwing the babysitter. I should divorce you just for being a cliché!"

"Divorce? Let's not rush into anything. What about some couples therapy?"

⋯⋯⟩ To agree to couples therapy, turn to 138.

⋯⋯⟩ To go ahead with the divorce, turn to 143.

⋯⋯⟩ To avoid the whole thing and run away to the airport, turn to 22.

"No, YOU are wrong," you write.
"No," comes the reply, "YOU are wrong."

┈┈⟩ To let this go, turn to 109.

┈┈⟩ To reply, turn to 6.

It's a match! Bartholomew invites you to his gentlemen's club. When you arrive, he says, "Thank God you're not ugly. You can never be sure with photo filters." He then talks in one breath about estate taxes, skiing in Vail, why women can't be sports commentators because their voices are too shrill, how much he loves gangsta rap, and Jordan Peterson. You wait in desperation for him to pause long enough for you to say that you are leaving. Four hours later, you are still there.

·····⟫ To try again for another match, turn to 86.

·····⟫ To delete the app, turn to 69.

Your husband and you spend weeks arguing about paint swatches. Eventually you narrow things down to 104 different colors that you paint samples of on your walls. Then you argue for several more weeks. You manage to eliminate one color. More arguing. Another color goes. More arguing.

It takes months, but you finally succeed in getting your choices down to two options:

⋯⋯⋗ Option one: Run away to Brazil! Turn to 34.

⋯⋯⋗ Option two: Get divorced! Turn to 143.

"Mom," you say, "I can't believe you're throwing Dad out, after all these years that he's put up with you! He's going to be really sad and lonely, and he probably doesn't even realize that he's better off without you!"

You go into another room and slam the door behind you. Then you call your dad's cellphone. As usual, he answers by loudly announcing his name.

"Dad, you know it's me, you just saw my name come up. You don't have to say your name."

"You might not know it's me."

"But I just called you. And it's your own phone. Dad. Are you OK? Mom told me what happened."

"Never better! You just caught me during the tea and cookies break at Senior Speed Dating at the community center. Did you know that on average men die younger than women, so at my age you can pretty much have your pick? And I have an extra advantage because I still have hair."

"Dad, I think you might be in shock."

"Not a bit of it! And I'm going to buy a motorcycle. I always wanted one but your mother wouldn't let me. Do you want to come with me to choose one?"

"Um—"

"Or come and keep me company while I get a tattoo!"

⋯⋯▷ To go motorcycle shopping with your dad, turn to 96.

⋯⋯▷ To go with your dad to get a tattoo, turn to 121.

You go with the shaman to his jungle retreat. The ceremonial space is a huge circular room with open walls and an ornately carved roof, with soft, colorful cushions and rugs strewn around, and plenty of incense burning.

"To hide the smell of vomit," explains the shaman.

A few pilgrims (tourists) linger, chanting, doing yoga stretches, and applying cream to their mosquito bites.

The shaman takes you down a path to a smaller building and unlocks the door. Inside is a ramshackle office space with a broken old sofa, an ancient computer, and piles of paper on every surface. It reminds you of every auto repair shop office you ever visited, except for the fact that the walls are covered with huge, tropical spiders. Once he gets the computer to work, you take him through Excel, and he tells you that before he was a shaman he worked in a store selling vacuum cleaners. He prefers being a shaman.

When the lesson is over, he asks whether you want your ayahuasca experience now.

·····⟩ Yes, you do! Turn to 21.

·····⟩ Absolutely not! Turn to 87.

The builders are back, and explain to you that the fire damage is really bad but luckily your house has been saved. It now needs redecorating from top to bottom. They hand you some paint swatches.

You have burned up your home and all of your possessions and you still have to decide between Victorian Underwear and Baby's Eyelash. You will be redoing your kitchen forever. As you collapse with a panic attack in the middle of the paint store, you wonder how you ended up here.

You call up your ex-husband. After a bit of small talk and a surprisingly vicious argument over the current location of the multiheaded screwdriver, you gently suggest the notion of having another baby together.

"It might be exactly what we need to bring us back together," you say.

There is a long silence.

"OK," he says, "but mainly because dating is terrible and I can't afford the rent on a one-bedroom apartment."

A year later you are sitting up in bed trying to get a hysterical baby to latch on to your breast while your ex-husband (you have not bothered to get remarried) somehow manages to snore beside you. You still don't know where the multiheaded screwdriver is. You know where you are, though, and you wonder how you ended up here.

You manage to sit with your foot behind your head for twenty minutes while the paramedics come and take away a woman who dislocated her hip. You have discovered the miracle of yoga. Nothing has ever spoken to you this deeply before.

You abandon everything else in your life to train as a yoga teacher. It's such an incredible practice that has the power to reach out across all boundaries and embrace the life force in all people. And you feel such a sense of community. All the other teacher trainees are midlife women exactly like you.

You do yoga for several hours every day. You practice mindfulness, equanimity, and nonviolent communication. You become vegan. You are grounded, centered, and whole. You have eliminated negativity from your life.

One day you are in Lululemon furnishing your soul and you get into a fistfight with a total stranger over the last Feel Your Release Uplifting Tank Bra. As you pull out a clump of her hair and she spits in your eye, you wonder how you ended up here.

You have never been in a tattoo parlor before. The tattoo artist looks about fifteen.

"How long have you been doing tattoos for?" you ask him.

"Twelve years," he says.

So OK, he is probably older than fifteen.

Your dad is browsing designs. He pauses over a skull with a rose in its teeth, a naked lady, and a snake wrapped around a heart, before showing the tattoo artist an abstract symbol.

"What does that mean?" he says.

"Eternal life," says the tattoo artist.

"Oh, that one definitely," says your dad. He has always been an optimist.

The tattoo artist inks the symbol on your dad's back while you do the *Times* crossword together.

"How about you?" says your dad when his is finished. "I'll treat you if you like."

⋯⋯▷ To get a tattoo, turn to 147.

⋯⋯▷ To turn down your father's kind offer, turn to 3.

You open your Twitter account. Two and a half hours later, you have read a lot of articles about perimenopause, and a lot of articles about celebrity divorces, and you definitely know which character in *The Good Place* you are. Suddenly, you see a tweet you do not like. Somebody has insulted national treasure Betty White.

⋯⋯⋗ To give this person a piece of your mind, turn to 6.

⋯⋯⋗ To let it go, turn to 109.

You get home. If anyone noticed that you'd almost run away to Brazil, they are polite enough not to mention it.

That evening you are on Twitter and you notice that everyone is retweeting a hilarious thread. It's been posted by an anonymous airport official and it is the story of a ridiculous middle-aged woman who messed up her life and nearly ran away to Brazil but then was too pathetic even to do that. Everybody wants to know who this ridiculous middle-aged woman is.

Within forty-eight hours you are being besieged by the press. Soon there are so many TV cameras surrounding your house that you can't go outside.

As you hide with the curtains closed and the lights off, your phone rings. It is someone from the office of the president. Before you have time to wonder how they got your number, they explain that the Brazilian ambassador has been complaining about how you insulted the great nation of Brazil by refusing to go there, and that you must issue a formal apology.

As you cower in the back of a car with blacked-out windows that has been sent to take you to the Brazilian embassy, trying to figure out how to explain that the problem isn't Brazil, it's you, you wonder how you ended up here.

God, nightclubs are loud. You try to remember when you last went to one. You are pretty sure there are people here who weren't even born then. It's fun, though. You feel sad that you stopped going dancing. You used to go to clubs all the time. Then there was a stretch of about ten years when you had to go to a wedding every weekend, so you stopped going to clubs, but that didn't matter because you were dancing at the weddings. Eventually everyone was married, so the weddings stopped, and by then you had a daughter, so anything that involved leaving the house and staying up late fell somewhere between insanity and impossibility. Even then you still danced around your kitchen, until your daughter got old enough to find that excruciatingly embarrassing and started yelling at you every time you did it. You still do it, mainly because embarrassing your daughter is fun, but it's not the same.

You've been throwing your best shapes on the dance floor for a while when you realize that someone is dancing with you. He's young and he's hot and he's a really good dancer. At first you think it's coincidence and he's just dancing nearby, but no, he is definitely dancing with you. He makes eye contact and then he takes your hand.

He yells a question. You can't hear him. He yells it again. You still can't hear him. He yells it a third time. You still can't hear him and you can't ask him to yell it again. So you say yes. You have no idea what you've just agreed to.

Toss a coin!

⋯⋯⟩ If it's heads, turn to 90.

⋯⋯⟩ If it's tails, turn to 18.

It's a match! You arrange a date. You ask him for another photo so you can spot him, but he just sends you more group pictures taken in bars. You figure that at least he will recognize you. You arrive at the pub that Gus suggested only to find it full of men who look exactly like Gus, or at least, exactly like all of the men in Gus's profile picture: plump cheeks, little eyes, rounded nose, thin lips, bald or with shaved heads. You had never registered before just how many men in the world look like potatoes. You approach each of these men and ask whether they are Gus, but none of them are. You get a drink and sit down alone. You wait. Gus does not show up. You text him but you get no reply. You have gone from all men being Gus to no men being Gus.

⋯⋯> To try again for another match, turn to 38.

⋯⋯> To delete the app, turn to 69.

"Fantastic!" says Mrs. Hot Russell. "What's your number?"

A week later, you are stripping at Hot Russell's Not So Hot Brother-in-Law's fiftieth birthday party. It is awkward and humiliating but it's still better than admitting to Mrs. Hot Russell that you were at a sex club with her husband (who is now recovering but still has anxiety attacks when he sees rubber gloves). Afterward, four people ask you for your rates and availability.

You are now a MILF stripper. Soon you have more bookings than you can handle and have to hire some other women to share the workload. Within a year, you win an award for being one of the best employers of working mothers in the country. You land a judging slot on the new late-night reality show *Stripping with the Stars* and become embroiled in a public feud with the head judge of *The Great American Clothes Off* over your differing opinions on nipple tassels. Your husband is delighted by the additional income and the fact that you practice all your routines on him, but your daughter is so embarrassed that she has to change schools and her name. As you offer your critique on Ryan Seacrest's booty shimmy on the *Stripping with the Stars* Christmas special, you wonder how you ended up here.

No, but I'm about to. Look away now, you type to Hot Russell. Then you open up the picture, do some cropping, and send it to your husband.

It occurs to you that nothing is stopping you from sending it to Hot Russell as well.

······⟩ If you decide to send the picture to
Hot Russell, turn to 30.

······⟩ If you decide to wait for your
husband's reply, turn to 7.

You are in the restroom in a conference center in an industrial park and indescribably terrible things are happening to your body. You didn't realize that the "holistic emotional purge" was going to be quite so literal. In the brief moments between spasms you reflect on the fact that for the same amount of money you spent on this retreat you could have taken a weeklong package vacation in Hawaii and you wonder how you ended up here.

You take over pushing the gigantic pile of luggage while the old lady thanks you profusely. You feel the warm glow of virtue, right up until the sniffer dogs start congregating around you. You look around. The very little, very old lady is nowhere to be seen.

Admit it: You knew this was going to happen.

You have plenty of time to reflect on your own stupidity as you are taken away to jail.

·····> Turn to 27.

It feels like forever before your husband replies. You are about to complain to Hot Russell that your sexting isn't working when a message finally pops up on your screen.

Feel like taking the rest of the day off? it says, followed by the winking face and the eggplant emoji.

You have nothing scheduled for after this meeting.

·····⟩ To wait out the meeting and then go home, turn to 40.

·····⟩ To tell your boss that this meeting is a complete waste of time, turn to 4.

You text Hot Russell:

Anything you want to share with the class?

His phone buzzes and you see the look of surprise as he reads your message. He glances at you, and then types a reply. A moment later, it arrives.

Just a bit of sexting to pass the time.

You feel a stir of excitement in your belly. You haven't felt excited in a meeting since the time that the vice president of marketing got an epic nosebleed all over a box of donuts.

Another message pops up on your screen.

Have you ever done it?

As it happens, you have never done it, but you and your husband have often talked about it. It is your husband's dream that you would send him a picture of your boobs while he is having a client meeting, and you happen to know that he is having a client meeting this morning. You actually have a picture of you with your boobs out, taken when sunbathing topless on vacation three years ago in Spain. Your daughter is in the picture, making a sandcastle in the bottom right-hand corner, but you could crop that out.

On the other hand, your husband is very familiar with the appearance of your boobs. Hot Russell is not.

·····⟩ To send your husband a picture of your boobs, turn to 127.

·····⟩ To send Hot Russell a picture of your boobs, turn to 30.

You awaken on a couch in a small office overlooking the parking lot while a seven-foot-tall man covered in cosmic tattoos puts Tiger Balm under your nostrils.

"Some people just aren't ready for enlightenment," he says.

He explains that you have to leave the facility because your presence is distracting the other seekers. He really uses the word "seekers."

On the way home you stop for gas at the rest area off the highway. As you sit in a Starbucks eating a limp ham sandwich that you can't taste because your nose is on fire, you wonder how you ended up here.

The more you read about cryptocurrencies, the more it seems like it would be madness not to invest all of your savings in them. It is literally a license to print money. You consider consulting your husband, but that would mean explaining what got you to this point. You decide it would be a better idea to surprise him. Surely, this is why you got a joint bank account in the first place.

You do have a few questions, though. It's not really a problem that you can only spend your cryptocurrency online, because you do most of your shopping that way anyway, but with some of these currencies, each of the cryptocoins are so expensive, you could put your life savings into them and still only end up with about four coins. So when you want to spend them, how do you get change?

As you are pondering these issues, a pop-up box appears on your computer and a friendly stockbroker offers to help you with your decision-making.

⋯⋯⟩ To take the broker's advice, turn to 95.

⋯⋯⟩ To ignore the broker, turn to 8.

"I'm a strip-a-gram," you tell Mrs. Hot Russell. "Russell's colleagues hired me to come and cheer him up, but he was asleep, so it didn't go very well."

The nurse stifles a laugh but she doesn't say anything. God bless nurses.

"Wow," says Mrs. Hot Russell, "I didn't know people stripped with your age and body type. That's really empowering. Do you do parties?"

·····⟩ To tell Mrs. Hot Russell that, why yes, you do do parties, turn to 126.

·····⟩ To cut your losses and tell Mrs. Hot Russell the truth, turn to 65.

"I'm sorry, Cheryl," you say. "I've been under a lot of stress recently . . . ," *ever since you laid off half my team even though their jobs were necessary and then gave all of their work to me to do, you add in your head.*

"I see," says Cheryl. "Well, you're obviously not much use in your current state, so maybe you should take the rest of the day off and then come back in refreshed on Monday morning. I recommend that you stop by Human Resources on your way out, to talk through your difficulties handling stress . . . ," *and so they can recommend some pointless relaxation techniques while I do nothing to relieve your workload, you add in your head.*

⋯⋯▷ To go straight home, turn to 40.

⋯⋯▷ To go to Human Resources, turn to 84.

"Hot Russell!" you exclaim.

"What?" says Hot Russell.

"Er, I mean just Russell. What are you doing here?"

"Same thing you are, I imagine."

"Oh. Right. So . . . do we have sex now?"

"Who said anything about sex? I'm getting a rash. I think I'm allergic to latex."

You examine Hot Russell's naked body and he does indeed have a rash, which is getting more virulent every second.

"I feel faint," says Hot Russell. And he passes out.

·····∴ Turn to 41.

"Which one is the dating site for people who want casual sex?" says your mother. "Is it Grindr?"

"Mom! First of all, *you* can't go on Grindr. Secondly, what do you mean, casual sex?"

"Darling, I haven't had sex with anybody other than your father for fifty years, and for quite a lot of that time not even with him. I'm not looking for a new relationship. At my age all I'm going to find is some old fart who'd rather get a new wife for free than pay for an old people's home. I just want to have some fun."

"But I don't think there is a website for old people who want to have casual sex."

"Well, there should be," says your mother.

So the two of you decide to set up a website for old people who want to have casual sex. You call it Fifty Shades of Gray Hair. It is hugely successful. Your mother and you both become very wealthy internet entrepreneurs, but sometimes, particularly when you are looking at some of the photographs people post on the site, you wonder how you ended up here.

You are actually looking forward to couples therapy. At last, someone will tell your husband everything that he is doing wrong! You tell your husband everything that he is doing wrong all the time, of course, but it will be nice to have someone agree with you.

Then you go to couples therapy. To your horror, the therapist does not spend all his time telling your husband what he is doing wrong. Instead, he spends a lot of time telling you what *you* are doing wrong. This is not what you signed up for at all! He lets you talk some of the time, but he also forces you to listen to your husband. Sometimes he even says that your husband is right. It is extremely annoying.

⋯⋯⟩ To give up on couples therapy and get a divorce, turn to 143.

⋯⋯⟩ To persist with couples therapy, turn to 58.

You explain to the police officers the circumstances of your life. They agree that the logical response to this is, indeed, to run away to Brazil. In fact, they can't understand why you changed your mind, but they agree to let you go.

┈┈⫶⟩ To change your mind again and get on the flight to Brazil, turn to 34.

┈┈⫶⟩ To go home, turn to 123.

Everyone in the dynamic meditation room is given a plastic bucket, a roll of paper towels, and a large foam block to punch.

"You never know what is going to emerge," explains the dynamic meditation leader, who goes by the name Shanti Mandala Om, which you suspect is not the name her parents gave her.

She talks you through what to expect from the meditation.

Ten minutes of hyperventilating.

Ten minutes of full-body shaking.

Ten minutes of hopping on one leg shouting "Hup."

Ten minutes of hopping on the other leg shouting "Hup."

Ten minutes of "expelling whatever wants to come out." Shanti Mandala Om encourages you to just "go with the flow."

Ten minutes of standing completely still with your arms in the air.

Ten minutes of ecstatic dancing.

Ten minutes of lying on the floor in the fetal position, softly weeping.

Then she puts on some incredibly loud sitar music and the meditation begins.

After two minutes of hyperventilating, you faint.

······⫶ Turn to 132.

You run away from your office down the street. You have not gone very far but you are already pretty sure this was a bad idea. Passersby stare at you and you smile at them and hope that they think you are out for a nice jog but you know this is unlikely given that you are wearing a business suit and high heels, which are beginning to hurt.

You need to decide where you are running to.

⋯⋯> To go home, turn to 40.

⋯⋯> To go to your parents', turn to 104.

⋯⋯> To go to the airport, turn to 22.

You talk to your best single friend about the process. She tells you that it's pretty straightforward to get donor sperm, although it's insanely expensive for something that teenage boys literally flush down the toilet probably several times a day. You're also amazed by how much you have to pay to get someone to whack it up you—how hard can it be? Still, compared with the cost of actually raising a child, it's peanuts. You go back to the leering doctor and have some tests and you discover that you're lucky and don't need IVF, "despite your age," he tactfully adds. You get drunk with your best single friend (which is to say, you get drunk and she doesn't, because of the IVF) and you go through the catalog of donors. This is the first time you have bought something from a catalog since you ordered a stereo when you were fifteen. You choose a sperm donor whose description sounds like you in the hope that the baby won't look completely random. You make an appointment for the insemination. You put up with the unpleasant process and the horrible doctor's horrible jokes.

And then you wait . . .

Toss a coin!

·····⟩ If you get heads, turn to 152.

·····⟩ If you get tails, turn to 49.

143

You are in the office of your divorce lawyer. She reminds you of Cruella de Vil, but not as nice.

She drawls: "The key thing is to fight him hardest for the things he wants but you don't care about, so that when you finally concede, you can get disproportionately more of the things you actually want without him even noticing."

"I don't think he's going to believe I want the PlayStation," you say.

"Oh, and don't ask for full custody of the kid. I know you think you want her now, but once the victory has worn off, you'll wish you'd secured yourself more free time. This man is no longer your husband. From now on you need to think of him as free babysitting."

She is terrifying, and you almost feel regret, but then you remember your husband's—sorry, your free babysitter's—fungal toenails.

You are now single! What's your first move?

⤑ To install a dating app, turn to 60.

⤑ To call your best single friend, turn to 63.

"Of course I'm not sleeping with Annika!"

You scrutinize your husband and decide that he's telling the truth. He is incapable of lying convincingly, which you know from every time he compliments your mother's cooking. And anyway, there is no way that Annika would sleep with him. You've had years to acclimatize to his paunch as it slowly developed, but if someone that young and beautiful were exposed to it all at once, it might actually blind her. You need to protect them both from this turn of events.

"What about if you didn't screw Annika, but I learned Swedish? Or studied physics? And then we can role-play in bed."

"That might work," agrees your husband. He sounds relieved, possibly because now he doesn't have to make a pass at someone who understands mirror neurons and can identify most of the current Top-40 singles, if indeed singles are still a thing.

⋯⋯▷ To study Swedish, turn to 44.

⋯⋯▷ To study physics, turn to 93.

It's a great plan, especially as you have been paying home insurance your entire adult life and never once filed a claim. That'll teach the insurance companies to raise their premiums every year! Haha, suckers!

You don't want anybody to get hurt, though, so you wait until this year's neighborhood block party for the Fourth of July. You make sure that all of your neighbors are outside eating mini burgers and drinking warm beer and then you sneak back to your house.

You have never set fire to a house before and you couldn't find a YouTube how-to video, so you are going to have to improvise. You don't have any gasoline lying around—who has gasoline lying around?—but you do have plenty of vodka, so you pour the vodka all over the place (including some down your throat) and then you light it with a kitchen match, which is about the only functional thing left in the kitchen.

It works. Your house is now on fire.

You go back to the party and dance to a Spotify "hits of the '80s and '90s" playlist until the flames get big enough that someone notices and calls the fire department.

Toss a coin!

┈┈┈> If you get heads, turn to 118.

┈┈┈> If you get tails, turn to 62.

Shay, the wellness and nutrition adviser, is slim and muscular with a shaved head and a lot of eye makeup. In front of you is a long table, with a stack of binders at one end and lots of unlabeled bottles of liquids at the other end. The colors of the liquids vary from venomous green to sludge.

Shay encourages everyone to pick up a binder and talks you through the basics. From now on, you are only allowed to eat for six hours a day, five days a week. (You are not obligated to eat for the entire six hours.) Subsections of the binder break down foods into categories including inflammatory foods, FODMAPs, nightshades, high-GI foods, and trans fats. You are not permitted to eat any of these foods. At the very back of the binder there is one sheet of paper listing foods that you are allowed. "Obviously, you should only eat organic, biodynamic versions of these foods, when in season. And I'm afraid that list is slightly out of date, so please cross off the following items." They list twelve foods, all of the ones on the list that taste of something. "It's important not to overtax your taste buds," they add.

Now Shay introduces you to the juices, which you are allowed to drink on your fast days. They talk at length about the differences between spirulina and chlorella, and you get sleepy, perhaps because you have been eating too many nightshades. At last, they invite you to sample a juice. Which do you choose?

······⋗ To drink the venomous green juice, turn to 29.

······⋗ To drink the sludge juice, turn to 100.

You decide to have a tattoo on your ankle. You look through the designs. After a false start where you accidentally choose something that people have tattooed onto them if they have done an Iron Man (you have not done an Iron Man, you don't even iron), you pick out a design that you mostly like because it's really small.

"It means courage," says the tattoo artist.

"Perfect," you say.

It turns out that having a tattoo REALLY hurts. You change your mind. You don't want a tattoo after all. You ask the tattoo artist to stop.

"But I've only done half of it!"

"I don't care."

"It'll look weird."

"I'll wear socks!"

Every morning as you pull your socks up over the half tattoo meaning courage on your ankle, you wonder how you ended up here.

It's a match! You send Night Tiger a friendly text and he replies *COME HERE PRINSESS I WILL GIVE YOU HOT NITE*. You appreciate his directness. Also his torso was pretty buff, even with the toothpaste marks. Let's face it, you did not swipe right for any other reason. You go over to his apartment, which is above a kebab shop. He starts to talk but somehow you can hear the spelling mistakes in what he is saying so you shut him up by sticking your tongue in his mouth. He carries you to the bedroom. You've always wanted somebody to do that. His sheets smell of tzatziki. You try not to think about when they were last changed. You allow him to give you a NIGHT OF PASHUN. You definitely use a condom. As you fall asleep, sated, in his arms, you hear the sound of two drunk women arguing in the street outside. You assume it is their puke you are tiptoeing over the next morning as you sneak off home.

That was fun but for some reason you don't see this person as a long-term prospect. You're not deleting his number from your phone, though.

⋯⋯⟩ To try again for another match, turn to 46.

⋯⋯⟩ To delete the app, turn to 69.